TEA, ITS MYSTERY AND HISTORY

Samuel Phillips Day, Lo Fong Loh

Secretary to the Chinese Educational Mission in Europe

1878

Lucius E. and
Elsie C. Burch, Jr.

This book or any portion thereof may not be reproduced or used in any manner whatsoever without the express written permission of the publisher except for the use of brief quotations in a book review.

Disclaimer and Terms of Use:

The Author and Publisher have strived to be as accurate and complete as possible in the creation of this book, notwithstanding the fact that she does not warrant or represent at any time that the contents within are accurate due to the rapidly changing nature of the contents and the Internet. While all attempts have been made to verify information provided in this publication, the Author and Publisher assume no responsibility for errors, omissions, or contrary interpretation of the subject matter herein. Any perceived slights of specific persons, people, or organization are unintentional.

Printed in the United States of America.

First Printing, 2019

Tea Trade Mart Publishing

800 NE Tenney Rd 110-429

Vancouver, WA 98685

www.teatrademart.com

Copyright © 2019 Jennifer C. Petersen

All rights reserved.

ISBN-13: 978-0-9984102-2-7

About the Author

JENNIFER C. PETERSEN

Jennifer Petersen lives alongside a creek in a quiet old-growth forest in the State of Washington. Her love of tea and history began in early childhood.

A member of the Specialty Tea Institute, she has been an STI Advisory Board member for over 12 years and is a Certified Tea Specialist.

With an extensive tea library and a fondness for pre-colonial history, Jennifer shares her insights with community groups and with fellow tea lovers.

Jennifer Petersen is a tea business development consultant and a masterful tea blender to the trade. She helps tea professionals start a tea business and she develops tea-training programs for food and beverage companies.

The director of Create+Design+Manage a Profitable Tea Business, Ms. Petersen is a professional trainer and STI Tea Mentor who conducts tea education seminars. Learn more at www.TeaTradeMart.com.

About the Editor

JENNIFER STOWE

Along with her three daughters, Jennifer Stowe owns and operates The Three Sisters' Tearoom in Campbellsville, TN and publishes tea-related books.

Jennifer is a Certified Tea and Etiquette Consultant, Herbalist and Registered Nurse who enjoys educating people on all aspects of tea.

Recently she founded the Mid-TN Tea Association which brings tea culture and tea lovers together all over Middle Tennessee by offering educational tea classes, workshops, tastings, tea travel and much more. In September, the association hosts the annual TN Tea Expo.

For more information please visit www.threesisterstearoom.com or contact Jennifer at midtntea@gmail.com.

Lo Fong Loh, C.I.C.S.
Secretary to the Chinese Educational Mission in Europe

**To the
Lovers of Pure Tea
this treatise
is respectfully inscribed.**

Contents

ABOUT THE AUTHOR 2

ABOUT THE EDITOR 3

Notes on the Chinese language 6

Extract from Mr. Lo Fong Loh's Journal 8

Chapter 1. Legendary origin of the plant 14

Chapter 2. Introduction of tea into England 24

Chapter 3. Appreciation of the leaf 32

Chapter 4. The plant botanically considered 35

Chapter 5. History of the tea trade 44

Chapter 6. The coloring of the leaf 51

Chapter 7. Social character of the beverage 54

Chapter 8. The "Drink of Health" 64

Chapter 9. The Virtues of the Leaf 69

Chapter 10. A CUP OF TEA 81

Notes on the Chinese language

The Chinese writing is eminently picturesque; and as the language admits of no alphabet, all ideas and objects are conveyed through the medium of groups of characters, each group representing a series of impressions, or opinions. By an ingenious and elaborate combination of strokes, upwards of 40,000 distinct symbols are perfected. This vast array has given rise to the amusing, but erroneous notion, the Chinese passed their lives in learning to read; so that old and infirm scholars, after having devoted all their days to its accomplishment, have departed this life with the task undone.

Idiographic and phonetic at the same time, the mechanism of the language is intelligible only to a few Europeans; but it is truly surprising that the vernacular of 400,000,000 of our fellow men, whose literature dates from the time of King David, and whose yearly exchange of merchandise with England amounts to £40,000,000, should have been so long wrapped in oblivion.

China does not possess, as we do, public libraries and reading rooms, but all who have a taste for reading or desire instruction can readily satisfy their need, as books are sold in the Celestial Empire at prices lower than in any other country in the world; further, all the finest quotations from the best authors are found written on the pagodas, public monuments, façades of tribunals, signs of the shops, doors of houses, and interior of apartments, so that, in fact, China may be likened to a huge library, rich and poor alike can enjoy their countries literature, and it is deserving of remark that the general prosperity and peace of China has been much promoted by the diffusion of knowledge and education throughout the lower classes.

The construction of the Chinese symbols varies from the square character to the more cursive character of the Seal and Grass, peculiar for their obscurity. The six styles of writing are as follows: Cuen shoo, or Seal character; Le shoo, or Official character; Keae shoo, or Model character; Hing shoo, or Running character; Tsaov shoo, or Grass character; and Sung shoo, of Sung dynasty character. The preface to this book is written by Lo Fong Loh, Esq., in the "running" character, and is undoubtedly a perfect specimen of calligraphy; his translation is rendered in the following pages.

Extract from Mr. Lo Fong Loh's Journal

Among the several places of interest in London, visited by H. E. Li Fung Pao (Director of the Chinese Educational Mission) and myself during our six months sojourn therein, I could not fail to be impressed with the Tea Establishment of Messrs. Horniman[i] and Co., Wormwood Street. The first department to which her attention was directed, is called the "Blending Floors". Here we observe diverse descriptions of tea, which had been shipped from different countries in the Eastern Hemisphere. Although we do not profess to be au courant with regard to that particular article of domestic use, still we happened to come from the tea districts of China, and therefore took the opportunity of examining some specimens of the tropical leaf.

We are aware that in commerce there is a special kind of so-called Tea, denominated "Reviving Leaf", a spurious production, so colored and prepared as to deceive the eye of all but experts. This manipulated "presentment" of the genuine commodity was not among the varieties; we are satisfied that Messrs. Horniman's Teas are perfectly unsophisticated and natural growths, free from all adventurous "additions". The effect of blending the various descriptions of tea is to make the flavor uniform, and thus to meet the wants and tastes of the consumers.

One thing particularly struck us during our visit. This was a vast quantity of tea in stock, both in the warehouses and the wholesale establishment. Upon inquiring of the head of the firm, whether all their importations are consumed by the people of the United Kingdom, the reply was, that "a considerable portion thereof is exported to European countries". This circumstance convinced us that the teas are blended with marked technical skill, in order to sooth the various tastes and likings of diverse individuals and nationalities.

When H.E. Li and I were passing through the "Blending Floors", the first remark made to me by H.E was this: he observed that "in China, tea merchants invariably separate the different qualities of the leaf; while the practice in this country seem to be the very reverse". I explained to him the reason of such usage, comparing it to the composition of the book. First, you collect information of sundry kind; anon, proceed to classify the same; and, finally, artistically blend the whole for the general advantage. The Chinese merchants having performed the first part, Messrs.

Horniman & Co. effect the other equally important portions.

Upon entering what is deemed the "Testing Room", we noticed a collection of tiny China cups, filled with infusions of the leaf. Albeit we did not then taste the tempting liquid, nevertheless we could not avoid being favorably impressed with the delicate aroma and excellent color of the beverage.

SORTING TEA

Great care is bestowed on the finest chops (grades) of tea to sort out all defective leaves; this work requires considerable practice and application.

The next apartment we inspected was the "Weighing Floors", which proved no less a source of interest. In this place, the tea is weighed previous to its being put into packages, varying in size from 2 ounces to several pounds weight. While the smaller packages are neatly enclosed in tinfoil, so as to prevent the leaf suffering injury through the action of damp or exposure, the larger sorts and for export are done up in tins, securely closed, to obviate the admission of air.

In the adjoining department, or "Labeling Room", the various packages are labeled (the labels being printed in nine languages) on a similar principle to that adopted by the Chinese themselves.

Shortly after my arrival in England, I felt distressed respecting the means of procuring pure tea, not drinking colored tea in my own country. I experience that some of the largest hotels and leading restaurants seldom produced a beverage such as I could with pleasure drink. Upon trying the tea supplied by Messrs. Horniman's Agents, I found it excellent in every respect, and like to that I have been accustomed to use when at home.

One object of my official visit to Europe being to collect special information bearing on the Industrial Arts, as evidences of Western civilization, I must confess that both H.E. Li and I derived mutual pleasure and profit in going over Messrs. Horniman's Establishment.

    LO FONG LOH

    London, May 1878

Chapter 1. Legendary origin of the plant

According to the most authentic Chinese historians, the tea plant was introduced from the Corea in the Eighth century, during the dynasty of Lyang. Being both approved of and much relished by the Emperor, it was extensively cultivated and it rapidly became popular with all sections of the community. As the story was too prosaic for general acceptance, the masses, and even certain skeptical literati, readily received a more poetical account, which, like many of our own nursery tales, veils some political allegory.

The story runs, that in the year 510, an Indian Prince – one Dharma, 3rd son of King Kosjusva - famed throughout the East for his religious zeal, landed in China on a missionary enterprise. He devoted all his time and thought to the diffusion of a knowledge of God. In order to set an example of piety to others, he imposed on himself various privations and mortifications, forgo sleep, and, living mostly in the open air, devoted himself to prayer, preaching, and contemplation.

Bodhidharma by Unkei Ikkei 1504-1520

Bodhidharma, Ukiyo-e woodblock print by Tsukioka Yoshitoshi, 1887

However, after several years in this excessively austere manner, he involuntarily fell asleep. Upon awaking, so distressed was he at having violated his oath that, to prevent a repetition of such backsliding and never again permit "tired eyelids" to "rest on tired eyes", he cut off those offending portions of his body and flung them on the ground. Returning next day to the same spot, he discovered that his eyelids had undergone a strange metamorphosis, having been changed into a shrub the like of which had never before been seen upon the earth.

Having eaten some of the leaves, he found his spirit singularly exhilarated thereby; while his former vigor was restored. Hence, he recommended the newly discovered boon to his disciples and followers, so that after a time the use of tea rapidly spread. A portrait of Dharma is given by Kaempfu, the first authoritative writer on China.

At the foot of the portrait is the representation of a reed, supposed to be indicative of the religious enthusiast having crossed rivers and seas in the pursuit of his mission. It is by no means difficult, out of this wonderful legend, to extract a moral, namely, that an earnest individual, who had acquired the useful habit of keeping his eyes open, discovered one of nature's secrets, which had entirely escaped the observation of all others.

Towards the close of the 16th century, a learned physician of Padua, one Giovanni Bolero, published a work "On the Causes of the Magnificence and Greatness of Cities". Therein, while treating of the Orient, he observes: "the Chinese have an herb out of which they press a delicate juice that serves them for drink instead of wine; it also preserves their health and frees them from all those evils which the use of wine produces among ourselves". Albeit the allusion is somewhat cloudy, still no doubt exists but that the celebrated Paduan refers to tea. This is supposed to be the earliest mention of the plant by any European writer.

It is curious that among the many wonderful things which Marco Polo – the great traveler of his day – saw in China, he omits to mention the tea plant either as shrub or beverage. This omission is the more unaccountable inasmuch as both himself and his father (whose voyages he records) must have visited districts wherein tea was in common use. The early Portuguese navigators are equally silent on this matter, nor is mention made thereof in the logs of our own freebooting Sea Kings. These, however, trouble themselves less about botany than the broad pieces to be found in the holes of the Spanish King's galleons. Had Sir Walter Raleigh, who traveled west instead of east, accompanied his friend Drake on his famous voyage around the world, he might have added to his discoveries of the potato and tobacco plants of America, that of tea in China. The honor of introducing the refreshing and invigorating leaf to Europe was, clearly, not reserved for English travelers. The Portuguese properly claims this honor, although they had been trading for many years with the Chinese before they made the discovery, just about the close of the 16th century.

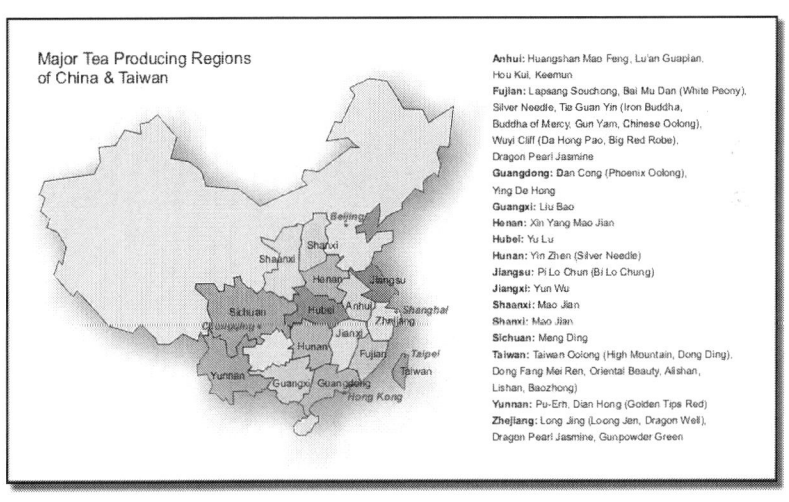

A TEA GARDEN

The tea plant flourishes best in the provinces of To-kien, Kiang-su, Hoonam, and Hoopels. The first crop is gathered in the early spring.

Shortly after tea had become a popular beverage in China, it was exported to Japan, the only nation with which the Chinese were suffered to hold intercourse. In those islands it assumed even a more important position than it held in the "Flowery Land", so that to be able to make and serve the beverage with a polished grace was recognized as an indubitable sign of a polite and aristocratic education.

The Japanese devoted their artistic and mechanical skill to the production of tea caddies, tea trays, teapots, and tea cups and saucers, remarkable for explicitness of design no less than peculiarity of fabric. Tea houses were open in the leading cities of Japan. These were frequented by the Daimios, or lesser nobles, and the lower classes alike, who took their chief pleasure in such popular resorts.

Eminent writers, also, consider that no indignity to extol the precious beverage. What Bacchanalian and hunting songs, cavalier, and sea songs, rhapsodical treatises in laudation of hunting, coaching, and so forth, are to the literature of England, such was tea to the writers, artists, and musicians of China and Japan.

In other words, their Dickenses, their Goldsmiths, their Nimrods, their Dibdins, their Tom Moores, and their Leeches, instead of having a wide variety of topics to treat of, as was the case with their English compeers, were confined to one subject – tea.

Indeed, each plantation was supposed to possess its peculiar virtues and excellences, like to the slightly varying Vineyards of the Rhine, the Rhône, the Garonne, or the Moselle. Each had its poet to sing its praises and running rhymes. In illustration, one Chinese bard, who seemingly was an Anacreon in his way, magnifies the shrub that grows on the Mong Shan mountains, and the territory of Ya-chew, in words which, literally translated, mean:

"One-ounce doth all disorders cure,

With two your troubles will be fewer;

Three to the bones more vigor give;

With four forever you will live,

As young as on your day of birth,

A true Isyen upon the earth".[1]

However hyperbolical this testimony may be considered, it at least serves to show the high estimation in which tea was held. This fact furnishes

---

[1] An immortal.

the best possible answer to the silly objections of certain modern writers who would fain have us believe that the Chinese cultivate tea, not for their own consumption, but to sell to foreigners.

The only gleam of truth latent and so manifestly absurd an assertion being that the Celestial's invariably drink the *pure* tea, not that which is undergone artificial preparation for those outer barbarians, the English consumers, it being an admitted fact that they prepare tea "to order," and can by the aid of mineral facing powder transform black tea into green, or green tea and black at pleasure. Such transformation, however, only alters the appearance to the eye; the quality, inferior or otherwise, remains concealed.

In due time tea became, not simply in China and Japan, but also in India and Persia, the drink of ceremony, just as his coffee with the Turks and Arabs and wine with us.

A little over two centuries since, a French traveler and Persia gravely imagined that what constituted a hospitable custom, was a universal desire to administer medicine. He avers that people "assigned to tea such extravagant qualities that, imagining it alone able to keep a man in constant health, they treated those who came to visit them with this drink at all hours".

This statement might be paralleled by an Eastern writer who, treating of England, should use the same sentence, merely substituting the word "wine" for "tea," and he may add, "to increase the beneficial influence of the beverage, in many instances they make cabalistic movements with the glasses sometimes clinking the edges together, meanwhile uttering the talismanic words, "Your Health!" which are supposed to possess some potent charm."

Chapter 2. Introduction of tea into England

Before tea found its way to England, it had been brought to Holland, thanks to the treaty made by the Dutch with the Japanese. If the Dutchman, as a rule, did not forgo his favorite lager and schnapps to take to tea so readily as did the English, nevertheless, there were not wanting upholders of the new beverage in the land of "Dykes, ducks, and Dutchmen", as somebody construed Voltaire's famous "cancana, canards, canaille".

The first to advocate the wonderful leaf was Cornelius Bontekoe, principal physician to the Elector of Brandenburg, a professor in the University of Leyden, and a man of more than ordinary eminence. In a treatise on "Tea, Coffee, and Chocolate", published in 1679, he strongly pronounces in favor of the first named drink, and denies the possibility of its being hurtful to health, even if taken in such in an inordinate quantity as 100 or 200 cups per day, a statement which is extravagant as it is impracticable.

The introduction of tea into England is by some presumed to date from the year of our Lord 1652. If such be authentic, the quantity of the leaf imported during the Commonwealth must have been extremely limited, probably not exceeding a few pounds, such as Blake and "sea dogs" of his order discovered in the cabins of ships they had captured from the Dutch. Equally questionable is the statement of other authorities, who give the year 1666 as that wherein the first importation of tea took place.

No doubt, many important events were commonly attributed to the year 1666, which the poet Dryden had essayed to render more remarkable still by his poem on the *Annus Mirabilis*. Lords Arlington and Orrery are credited with having first rendered the drinking of tea fashionable.

Six years previous to the remarkable year just noticed, Pepys records in his "Diary": "I sent for a cup of tea, a Chinese drink, of which I had never drunk before". So that it is evident the rare beverage was then coming into use. Shortly afterwards a measure passed the legislature, enacting that an impost of eightpence per gallon should be paid on all tea prepared and sold in coffee houses.

GATHERING THE SPRING CROP

The leaves are plucked, with great care, not more than one being plucked from the stalk at a time; notwithstanding this, an expert can gather 10 to 13 bs. per day.

A singular handbill was issued by Thomas Garway, the founder of Garraway's somewhat famous coffeehouse, in Exchange (subsequently Exchange – alley). This announcement was by chance discovered some years since in a volume of pamphlets in the "King's Library", British Museum, where it may still be inspected. Albeit the document bears no date, but there is ample internal evidence to prove that it had been printed about the year 1660. It purposes to be "an exact description of the growth, quality, and virtues of the leaf tea, by Thomas Garway, in Exchange-alley, near the Royal Exchange, in London, Tobacconist and Seller and Retailer of Tea and Coffee".

Subjoined is the quaint description given of the plant: –

"Tea is generally brought from China, and groweth there upon little shrubs and bushes, the branches whereof are well garnished with white flowers, that are yellow within, of the bigness and fashion of Sweetbriar, but in smell unlike, bearing their green leaves, about the bigness of scordium, myrtle, or sumac, and is judged to be a kind of sumac.

This plant hath been reported to grow wild only, but doth not; for they planted in their gardens, about 4-foot distance, and it groweth about 4-foot-high, and of the seeds they maintain and increase their stock. Of all places in China this plant groweth in greatest plenty in the province of Xemsi, latitude 36°, bordering upon the West of the province of Nanking, near the city of Luchow, the Island de Ladrones and Japan, and is called 'Cha'.

Of this famous leaf there are diverse sorts (though all one shape) some much better than others, the upper leaves excelling the others in fineness, a property almost in all plants; which leaves they gather every day, and drying them in the shade, or in iron pans over a gentle fire, till the humidity be exhausted, then put close-up in leaden pots, preserve them for their drink.

Tea, which is used at meals and upon all visits and entertainments in private families, and in the palaces of grandees; and it is owned by a padee of Macas, native of Japan, that the best tea ought to be gathered by virgins, who are destined for this work. "

"The said leaf is of such known virtues, that those very nations so famous for antiquity, knowledge, and wisdom, do frequently sell it among themselves for twice its weight in silver, and the high estimation of the drink made therewith hath occasioned an inquiry into the nature thereof amongst the most intelligent persons of all nations that have traveled in those parts, who after exact trial and experience by all ways imaginable, have commended it to the use of their several countries, and for its virtues and operations. The quality is moderately hot, proper for winter and summer. The drink is declared to be most wholesome, preserving in perfect health until extreme old age".

Then the writer proceeds at considerable length to enumerate the "Vertues" of tea, some of which are decidedly apocryphal. Amongst other properties attributed to the beverage are those of making the body active and lusty, helping the headache, giddiness, and heaviness, removing difficulty of breathing, clearing the sight, removing lassitude, strengthening the stomach and liver, causing good appetite and digestion, vanquishing heavy dreams, easing the frame, strengthening the memory, preventing sleepiness, "so that whole nights may be spent in study without hurt to the body," strengthening the inward parts and preventing consumption, especially when drunk with milk.

"And that's the virtues and excellencies of this leaf and drink," continues Mr. Garway, "are many and great is evident and manifest by the high esteem and use of it among the physicians and knowing men of

France, Italy, Holland, and other parts of Christendom, while in England it has been sold in the leaf for 6 pounds, and sometimes 10 pounds for the 1 pound weight; in respect of its former scarceness and dearness, it hath only been used as a regalia in high treatments, and presents made thereof to princes and grandees till the year 1657.

"The said Thomas Garway," so they handbill proceeds, "did purchase a quantity thereof and first publicly sold the said tea in leaf and drink, made according to the directions of the most knowing merchants and travelers in those Eastern countries, and upon knowledge and experience of the said Thomas Garway's continual care and industry in obtaining the best tea, and making drink thereof, very many noble men, physicians, and merchants, and gentlemen of quality, have ever since sent to him for the said leaf, and daily resort to his house in Exchange-alley aforesaid, to drink the drink thereof."

Finally the writer closes his remarkable encomium in these words: "and that ignorance nor envy may have no ground or power to report or suggest that which is here asserted of the virtues and excellences of this precious leaf and drink half more of design than truth, for its justification of himself and the satisfaction of others he hath here enumerated several authors who in their learned works have expressly written and asserted the same and much more in honor of his noble leaf and drink, viz.: – Bontius, Riccius, Jarricas, Almeyda, Horstius, Alvarez, Sameda, Marinivus in his *China Atlas*, and Alexander de Rhodes in *Voyage and Missions*, in a large discourse of the ordering of this leaf and the many virtues of the drink; printed at Paris, 1658, part X. Chapter 13.

And to the end that all persons of eminency, and equality, gentlemen and others, who have occasion for teas in leaf, may be supplied, these are to give notice that the said Thomas hath tea to sell from *16 to 50 shillings in the pound*".

Doubtless if the beverage possessed even but a tithe of the virtues and excellences attributed to it by the celebrated Garway it must be regarded as the crowning boon of Nature to man.

Chapter 3. Appreciation of the leaf

That the worthy Thomas Garway, to whom reference is made in the preceding chapter, gave rather undue license to his imagination in extolling the virtues of his cherished beverage is manifest. His handbill, however, is not only curious but interesting, if on no other account than that of illustrating the mode of advertising to which he resorted, in order to spread the fame of the precious leaf and dispose of his commodity. It is likewise noteworthy on account of the fame which "Garway's Tea" had acquired and maintained for two centuries.

The original name "Garway" was changed or "restored" by his son to "Garraway", while the House which bore this appellation became renowned far and wide. Here it was that the numerous schemes which surrounded and accompanied the great South Sea Bubble, had their center.

Appropriately enough also, "Garraway's" was the headquarters of the remarkable tea speculation of 1841-2, when prices fluctuated sixpence and eightpence per pound; and when people were suddenly smitten with the mania for dealing in tea, just as at other times a rage obtained for speculating in railways, mines, foreign funds, or finance.

Albeit Garway evidently prospered in his special branch of trade, yet it is probable that the rapid popularity which tea had acquired was less indebted to the "learned and knowing" authorities he quoted in his handbill, than to Royal patronage.

It appears that Catherine of Braganza, Queen of Charles II, who had tasted the beverage in Portugal, and grew enamored with the same, brought it into fashion in this country. Her fondness for the soothing cup was extreme.

Its subsequent popularity, however, may fairly be attributed to its innate valuable properties, which became the more understood and prized in proportion as the public grew more addicted to its daily use. Ladies of *ton* delighted in their "dish of tea", which was indispensable to their comfort.

Authors also discovered its advantages as a beverage to work upon; while poets and essayists lauded it well-nigh in terms of extravagant eulogy, such as had been employed by Chinese and Japanese men of letters before them.

Almost the first literary eulogist to espouse the cause of the new drink was Edmund Waller. He recites how he became induced to taste tea, owing to a parcel of the leaf being presented to him in the year 1664, by a member of the Jesuit Order, who had recently returned from China. In the poem which furnishes several references to the infuse leaf occurs the following pregnant allusion: –

"The Muses friend, tea, doth our fancy aid,

Repress those vapors which the head invade,

And keeps that palace of the soul serene".

Byron, in later times, became an enthusiast in its favor, averring that he "Must have recourse to black Bohea"; while he pronounces green tea "The Chinese nymph of tears".

Chapter 4. The plant botanically considered

The Linnaean system of botany classifies the tea plant with the *Polyandria,* end of the order *Monogynia.* What is style of the "Natural System" associates it with the family of the Camellia.

The tea plant, which is an Evergreen, grows to the height of five or six feet. The leaves are about an inch and a half long, being narrow, indented, and tapering to a point, similar to those of the Sweetbriar. The color is dark green.

The root is like that of the Peachtree, while the flowers resemble the wild Rose. A number of irregular branches issue from the stem. The fruit is small, containing round blackish seeds, about the size of a bean. The shrub must have at least a three years growth before it is fit for being plucked. This valuable plant is largely cultivated not only in China but also in India, Japan, and the Eastern Archipelago.

There are two primary kinds of tea, namely the *Thea Viridis,* or green shrub and the *Thea Bohea* or black plant. The former delights in elevated situations and a temperate climate; the latter requires the protection of valleys, the sloping sides of mountains, and the banks of rivers, with a more tropical sun. To the situations and the temperatures, the delicate flavor of the green and the greater astringency of the black tea are mainly due.

In England, at one period, all descriptions of black tea were denominated Bohea[2]. It is known, however, that this particular title belongs exclusively to inferior varieties, and in no way includes such superior products as Congou, Souchong, Pekoe, and I may add Caper, which is regarded as a fancy growth, and never imported into this country, unless adulterated.

Of the green teas, the commonest and cheapest is Twankay, the finest sort being Hyson, which comprises Young Hyson and gunpowder. There are a number of intermediate and less known varieties, to which must be added the fine growths of Assam and other provinces of British India.

The tea plant may be cultivated with more or less success in climates within 35° or 40° of the equator. Some writers affirm that so long as the temperature be suitable, the character of the soil is of little importance. Others, on the contrary, assert that tea will grow in any

---

[2] First mentioned in 1692; black tea once regarded as choicest but now an inferior grade; pronounced boh-hee.

part of China or India, even much further north than I have mentioned. The balance of experience, however, is against them.

Camellia sinensis flower

Sweet briar flower

WEIGHING

This illustration is from a photograph, showing the manner of weighing tea, and payment of wages. The leaf is subsequently prepared for firing.

As regards to the quality of tea, this must depend not only on its variety and growth but also on the time during which the leaves are gathered.

Directly the refreshing spring showers have passed off, and a gracious sunshine succeeds, which, aided by drying winds, chases away each leaflet's tears, the tea harvesting season commences with vigor.

Hundreds, and occasionally thousands, of little merry leaf gatherers may be seen sallying forth at early-morning to their pleasant labor, singing, laughing, prattling, and dancing as they go. Then when the midday gong sounds, work ceases for the nonce, when these pretty, black-eyed, dark-haired damsels squat in groups among the bushes, while they partake of their frugal meal of rice, moistened by copious draughts of hot weak tea. Immense care is necessary in order to protect the delicate young leaf from injury.

As a rule, the girls employed undergo a species of training to prepare them for their work. Not only so, but while engaged in plucking the flowery Pekoe, they wear gloves of perfumed leather. Every leaf must be plucked separately. Still so expert are the pluckers that an average gathering would amount to twelve pounds weight daily for each person.

There are three seasons. The first commences at the end of February, or the beginning of March; the second about the end of March, or the first week of April; third at the end of May, or in June. The earliest leaves constitute the most exquisite and expensive tea; while the second crop forms largest proportion of the entire produce.

The best description is the produce of the early spring when the leaves are young and small. But many growers, for the sake of increased quantity, preferred gathering the leaves later in the season, when they are not simply larger, heavier, and more numerous, but when they have lost much of their pristine flavor.

Of course, only experts, who devote their lives to the work, can distinguish the difference between the various growths of early spring or late autumn. Consequently, the ordinary consumer of tea is compelled to trust to the integrity of the particular retailer from whom he procures this commodity.

But as the majority of retail grocers do not profess to know the true value of tea, it follows that they in their turn, must place implicit trust in the better judgment of the wholesale dealer, commercial traveler, or middleman with whom they do business.

Tracing the history of tea to a very early period, we find that complaints of adulteration were very prevalent.

In England the chief deception practiced, consisted in the admixture of sloe[3] and other leaves with the genuine article. The re-drying of leaves that have been already used was a malpractice equally as disgraceful. The tea so tampered with was little better than a mass of woody fiber, destitute of those chemical properties upon the presence of which the value and virtue of this tropical beverage depend.

More mischievous still was the practice adopted sometimes since by which an ingenious mixture of sumac[4] leaves and catechu[5] was made to resemble tea so that ordinary persons could not detect the counterfeit. Yet, notwithstanding the last-mentioned substance, from its powerfully astringent action on the

---

[3] Prunus spinosa, called blackthorn or sloe, is a species of flowering plant in the rose family Rosaceae. It is native to Europe, western Asia and locally in northwest Africa. It is naturalized in New Zealand, Tasmania and eastern North America. Source: Wikipedia

[4] Sumac is a shrub or small tree of the cashew family, with compound leaves, fruits in conical clusters and bright autumn colors.

[5] Catechu, Acacia catechu, is a deciduous, thorny tree reputed for its polyphenol content.

system, was calculated to induce serious mischief to health, this objectionable compound was literally sold under the protection of a patent and was known in the trade as "La Veno Beno, the Chinese Tea Improver". The public, however, heard nothing of this impudent fraud, until after the scheme succeeded in all the mischief had been done.

Bad as are the adulterations of the leaf practiced in this country, those adopted by the Chinese are even worse. Not very long since, much commotion was created respecting "Lie Tea", which was thrust in the market. This "base presentment" consisted either wholly, or in great part, of leaves which had no affiliation whatever to the tea plant, but consisted of leaves and weeds gathered anyhow, then rolled and dried, and artificially flavored so as resemble the genuine article.

With reference to what is called green tea, the system frequently pursued in its preparation is highly reprehensible. The green tea sold in England are usually artificially colored in order to enamor the eye of the unsuspecting purchaser. The principal medium employed in effecting this result is none other than Prussian blue[6], a deadly poison, and inimical to health even in the minutest quantity. According to Mr. Fortune, no less a proportion than half a pound is used to every hundredweight of leaf.

Although botanists have divided tea into two species[7], still the black and green descriptions are but varieties of the same plant. Practically it is found more convenient to cultivate each sort separately, certain districts favoring the specific growths. But any description of black tea can, in the process of drying, be converted into green.

Of course, the Chinese never touch these artificially colored products. They have too much good sense for that. While they consider the English fools for their pains, because the pretty color tickles their fancy, and they are induced to pay a higher price for the sophisticated commodity.

---

[6] Prussian blue, potassium ferric hexacyanoferrate, is a dark blue pigment produced by oxidation of ferrous ferrocyanide salts. The Prussian Blue hex code is #003153

[7] Camellia sinensis assamica and Camellia sinensis sinensis.

Chapter 5. History of the tea trade

In 1658, the Honorable East India Company directed to be "sent home by their ships 100 pounds weight of the best tea they could get", this doubtless being considered a pretty large supply.

The company had previously presented to Catherine of Braganza, on her birthday, a chest containing 22 pounds – a notable gift commemorated by Waller. In 1671 came the Taiwan present from the Ruler of Bantam.

During the three subsequent years, the company bought of Mr. Thomas Garway and others 562 1/2 pounds of tea, which was either given away or consumed by the Court of Committee. From 1675 to 1677, no record exists of either purchases or imports. Hence, it is evident that tea was not regarded as a source of private revenue at that period.

Who could have fancied the marvelous change that a century or two would affect? Who could've thought that the tea trade was destined to become one of the most important branches of our commerce, and not only so, but to occasion several wars, lead to the extension of our Eastern possessions, and precipitate the great Chinese Exodus, which threatens such important results to the Pacific States of America, to Australia, the Polynesian Islands, and possibly to the world at large?

There is nothing in the history of commerce so marvelous as the growth and development of the trade and tea. In 1675, the importation of this commodity rose to 4713 pounds. But this enormous quantity manifestly overstocked the market for seven years afterwards.

In 1685, the importations amounted to a little over 12,000 pounds. Four years later, 25,000 pounds arrived, which caused the market to be glutted for a lengthened period, giving rise to considerable depression in that special branch of commerce.

About this period, the duty was taken off the "made" tea, and a regular impost of five shillings per pound imposed.

During the first twelve years of the 18th century, the total quantity of tea imported was 1,102,070 pounds, showing an average of 91,922 1/2 pounds. This result is the more remarkable as it exceeded the previously unheard-of quantity imported in 1700. Yet we find that in the eleven years succeeding, this amount became nearly doubled, probably owing to a reduction of duty to four shillings a pound, in addition to a Customs' impost 14%.

The tea trade, still ever augmenting, received a further impetus in 1746, when the duty was reduced to one shilling a pound, the Customs duty being fixed at 25%. During the following 12 years the average importation amounted to 2,558,080 pounds. Another period of eight year (1760-67) gives an average of 4,333,267 pounds.

Then taking an additional 10 years to complete the century, the first really commercial importation of 4,713 pounds in 1778, had grown to an average of 6,948,238 pounds, and this, notwithstanding that besides the 25% customs duty and the one shilling per pound excise impost, there had been imposed an additional excise 30%.

Further, in the concluding six years of the century, the tea importations had further augmented to 21,706,718 pounds, the 91,183 pounds of 1700 having become a century later upwards of *25 million pounds.*

In 1784, the Commutation Act passed the Legislature. By its provisions, the East India Company were compelled to make quarterly sales of tea, to sell even as low as one penny a pound above prime cost, and to keep a sufficient quantity for one year's consumption always on hand.

The same year Mr. Pitt reduced the duty to 12 1/2%, to which act ascribed the enormous increase in the trade. Although in 1795 the duty was raised to 20%, still the consumption of tea increased. Early in the 19th century other fiscal changes occurred. The Customs' duty, for example, was fixed at 6%, and the excise duty 90% in value; while in 1819 the former impost was repealed, and the latter made cent-per-cent.

However, nothing that statesmen or financiers could affect seem to check the growing fondness of English people of all social grades for their cherished beverage. Accordingly, we find that during the first 27 years of the 19th century – a period which completes the third 50 years of the tea trade – the average annual consumption amounted to about *29 million pounds.*

Since 1827, the intervening half-century has witnessed several fiscal changes in the tea trade.

The first and most important occurred in 1834, when the excise duty became removed, differential Customs' duties were imposed, and the long existing monopoly of the East India Company was abolished. In 1835, practically the first-year of free trade, the imports exceeded by 30% any previous period. The following year, at the request of the tea dealers and brokers, the differential duties were repealed, and a fixed impost of two shillings in the pound imposed, the result being an increase of importation to the extent of 50 million pounds. In 1840, a rate of 5% was charged, thus raising the duty to 2s. 2 1/4d. per pound.

Although the war with China, coupled with the simultaneous distress in the manufacturing districts, caused a temporary check to importation, still the conclusion of peace and the repeal of the Corn Laws had their due effect in an opposite direction.

Hence, in 1849, the quantity imported reached very nearly fifty-three and a half million pounds, while in the year of the first Great Exhibition, the importation had augmented to about seventy-one and a half million pounds.

In 1853, an act was passed reducing the duty immediately to 1s.6d. Five years later a reduction of 6d. took place, and again in June 1865, a further reduction. Since then no physical change has been affected. The effects of these fluctuations have been sufficiently marked, probably demonstrating that no further reduction, short of absolute abolition, would prove much of a boon to consumers.

DRYING

A basket frame, wide at both ends and contracted towards the center, containing the tea, is placed over hot embers of charcoal.

In 1861, the imports increased to 96 1/2 million pounds; the following year to close upon 115 million pounds, in 1863 to nearly 137 million pounds, and in 1866 to 140 million pounds, in 1877, to the enormous figure of nearly 88 million pounds (187,721,050 lbs. actually).

Thus in two centuries, since the time of Thomas Garway's handbill offering a few pounds of tea to a select public, the trade has grown with prodigious strides into a highly flourishing branch of commerce representing value to the extent of some 12 millions sterling, and an addition to the Imperial revenue at even the existing duty, of over 4 1/2 millions, irrespective of the value of the 32 million pounds re-exported from our shores.

Chapter 6. The coloring of the leaf

Before 1834, the Honorable East India Company, possessing the monopoly of the tea trade, were responsible, under very stringent regulations for the quality of the leaf imported, while heavy penalties were inflicted on those who colored or adulterated tea in England.

Now that the trade has been thrown open, and the duties so largely reduced, little inducement exists for having recourse to malpractices in this country, even had there been no Adulteration Act in force.

Yet is there no protection against what is done in China? Some years since, the City Commissioners made a commendable but abortive effort to seize "Lie Tea" and teas artificially colored and otherwise adulterated; but inasmuch as duty had duly been paid on the rubbish, it was found that nothing could be done to arrest the distribution of such vile stuff.

That the English public prefer unsophisticated tea, when they can conveniently obtain it, is conclusively established by Messrs. Horniman & Co.'s long experience. The Firm has agents in every town throughout the kingdom, each of whom is constantly receiving supplies of the genuine article. 10 years ago, the firm paid duty on *774,000 pounds of tea*, while last year they sold upwards of *5 million packets* varying in sizes from 2 ounces to 3 pounds weight.

This result is sufficiently conclusive and negating the flimsy assertion made and reiterated by interested persons, namely, that English folk favor artificially colored teas, rejecting those which are not so manipulated.

It must be admitted that inexperienced judges of the pure leaf, upon their first purchase are surprised at the color of the leaf. They pronounce the black tea to be dark brown, and the green tea, a dark olive.

The exquisite flavor of the "supreme beverage" at once opens their eyes to the truth. No doubt it is reassuring to be aware that a firm which, by common consent of their customers, consistently and persistently act up to their business formula, "Always good alike," find equitable reward in a yearly augmentation of their business; a fact attested by the published tables of the quantities of tea on which they pay duty periodically.

But in addition to obtaining *quality*, the public have the extra advantage of *cheapness*, as the pure tea offered by Messrs. Horniman & Co.'s Agents is sold at the same fixed prices in every Town and Village throughout the kingdom. If, as the proverb has it, "Good wine needs no bush[8]", so, on the other hand, good tea, like beauty, needs no adornment. Its best adornment is perfect purity.

ii

---

[8] The phrase *good wine needs no bush* means *there is no need to advertise or boast about something of good quality, as people will always discover its merits.*

It is first recorded in the epilogue to <u>As You Like It</u> by the English poet and playwright, William Shakespeare (1564-1616).

Chapter 7. Social character of the beverage

Since the introduction of tea into England, but more especially since the British public is patronized, a marked improvement characterizes the tone and manners of Society.

It is not, possibly, too great an assumption to assert that there must exist something about tea especially suitable to the English constitution and climate; for not even in Scotland or Ireland, nor in any European country, is the beverage consumed to a like extent.

Certain travelers aver that a large consumption of the leaf that is obtained in Russia; but it is chiefly the upper classes who are addicted to its use. The moujiks (Russian peasants) and artisans scarcely know the taste of it, for now, as in the time of Peter the Great, they regarded *vodka* as their only national drink.

FIRING AND COLORING

When the teas are half roasted, powdered Prussian blue, plumbago, gypsum, and turmeric are added, except to that tea ordered pure and free from all mineral facing powder.

That all classes of the community in this country have derived much benefit from the persistent use of tea, is placed beyond dispute. It has proved, and still proves, a highly prized boon to millions.

The artist at his easel, the author at his desk, the statesman fresh from an exhaustive oration, the actor from the stage after fulfilling an arduous role, the orator from the platform, the preacher from the pulpit, the toiling mechanic, the wearied laborer, the poor governess, the tired laundress, the humble cottage housewife, the votary of pleasure even, on escaping from the scene of revelry, nay, the Queen on her throne, have, one and all, to acknowledge and express gratitude for the grateful and invigorating infusion.

Shortly after it had become fashionable to partake of tea, persons of quality in England were wont to invite their friends to a "dish" of the newly imported beverage.

Lord Macauley mentions how "Tea, which at the time Monk brought the Army of Scotland to London (A.D. 1660), had been handed round to be stared at and just touched with the lips as a great rarity of China, was, 80 years later, a regular article of import, and was soon consumed in such quantities that financiers began to consider it as an important source of revenue."

Seven years later Pepys has this entry in his famous diary: "Home, and there find my wife making of tea, a drink which Mr. Pelling, the apothecary, tells her is good for her cold".

That Queen Anne ranked among the votaries of the leaf is manifest from Pope's couplet: –

"Thou, great Anna, whom three realms obey,
Dost sometimes counsel take, and sometimes Tay".

From this time forth writers of renown make constant allusions to the new drink. Essayists in the *Spectator*, the *Tatler*, and other literary organs, are ever-dropping remarks respecting the tea table. Pope, in his "Rape of the Lock", when Belinda is declaring what terrible thing she would rather have had happened, than have lost her favorite curl, makes her cap everything by the wish that she could be transported to

"Some isle
Where the gilt chariot never marks the way,
Where none learn ombre, none e'er drink Bohea",
– than which privation she can imagine nothing worse.

Then what a source of social pleasure the "afternoon tea" becomes! Brady, in his well-known metrical version of the "Psalms", thus illustrates the advantages accruing there from: –

"When in discourse of Nature's mystic powers
And noblest themes, we pass the well spent hours, whilst all around the Virtues – sacred band –
And listening Graces, pleased attendants stand.
Thus, our Tea conversations we employ,
Where with delight, instruction we enjoy,
Quaffing without the waste of time or wealth,
The sovereign drink of pleasure and of health".

The poet Cowper's praise of the beverage has been sadly hackneyed; nevertheless, as the Laureate of the tea table, his lines are worthy of further reproduction.

Who cannot recall how Mrs. Gilpin scornfully characterizes her neighbors' children as being markedly inferior to her own, "as hay is to Bohea"; as though the force of comparison could no further go? Yet it is in his more serious and didactic poem that the melancholy friend of the hares exclaims: –

"Now stir the fire, and close the shutters fast;
Let fall the curtain, wheel the sofa round;
And while the bubbling and loud hissing urn
Throws up a steaming column, and the cups,
That cheer, but not inebriate, wait on each,
So, let us welcome peaceful evening in."

But tea had its avowed enemies no less than its staunch friends. Certain old-fashioned physicians not like it. Nay, they even sneered at and denounced it.

Jonas Hanway, the philanthropic but eccentric founder of the Marine and the Magdalene societies, bolder than his compeers, actually rushed into print in order to inveigh against it. But he had reason to regret his hotheaded impetuosity. In answer to his petty attack, the beverage found a noble defender in no less a personage than Dr. Johnson, whose defense, in point of style, is among the best essays the great moralist ever penned. Hanway, however, nothing daunted, resumed the attack.

Having lost his temper, he gave full scope to his prejudices, and denounced tea as the worst of poisons and the secondary cause of all the moral, religious, and political evils that distracted mankind. Not only so, but he was rash enough to attack the leviathan and of literature personally. Yet he had far better have saved his ink, for Johnson – the first time in his life that he had retorted on an adversary – fell upon him like an avalanche.

Hanway having foolishly laid himself open to ridicule, most assuredly the Doctor did not spare him. Such a contest, of course, could not be regarded as equal. No possible comparison existed between the combatants.

Therefore, setting aside all the hard knocks which Johnson administered the poor Jonas, it will be sufficient to produce one passage in which the eminent writer declares himself "a hardened sinner in the use of the infusion of this plant, whose teapot had no time to cool, who with tea solaced the midnight, and with tea welcomed the morning."

There is not the slightest exaggeration in this confession. What is affirmed therein is attested both by Boswell and Mrs. Thrale in their respective writings, who record that Dr. Johnson frequently exceeded a dozen large cups at one meal.

It is alleged that the first command given by our gracious Queen upon her accession to the throne was "Bring me a cup of tea and *The Times*". It is to be hoped that Her Majesty got the former uncolored.

Victoria (Alexandrina Victoria; 24 May 1819 – 22 January 1901) was Queen of the United Kingdom of Great Britain and Ireland from 20 June 1837 until her death. On 1 May 1876, she adopted the additional title of Empress of India.

Her reign of 63 years and seven months was longer than that of any of her predecessors and is known as the Victorian era. It was a period of industrial, cultural, political, scientific, and military change within the United Kingdom, and was marked by a great expansion of the British Empire.

For a time, it appeared that so far as one class of the community was concerned, the use of tea was likely to be checked by the imperious sway of inconstant fashion.

It became the custom in the houses of the aristocracy to supply only coffee after dinner, so that, for a period, tea was ostracized. Recently however, a reaction has set in, for we find that the most agreeable meetings in "Society" are those which assemble at "the 5 o'clock tea".

Accordingly, one of the whirligigs of time has so conspired, that while the fashionable breakfast and dinner hours are completely revolutionized, the hour for tea has reverted to the precise period of the day at which it used to be taken 100 years ago.

Although noble ladies have not now black pages to hand round the teacups, yet the very china used by their great-grandmothers is called into requisition simply because of its antiquity. One circumstance calls for special notice.

It is this, that in the words of Dr. Johnston[9] "Everywhere un-intoxicating and nonnarcotic beverages are in general use among tribes of every

---

[9] Chemistry of Common Life.

color, beneath every sun, and in every condition of life. The custom, therefore, must meet some universal want of our common nature".

Philanthropists and sociologists are now fully alive to the moral effects produced by such non-intoxicant drinks as tea and coffee. Intemperance is the bane of the nation. And now that legislation has utterly failed to restrain the evils arising therefrom, philanthropy, full of faith in the experiment, endeavors by the establishment, in divers quarters, of quite a different class of "Public Houses", to arrest an evil which is assuming the gravest character.

And there can be no doubt that if the masses could be induced to substitute the pure beverages tea and coffee for the deleterious fluids, they are wont to imbibe, the salutary change would vastly benefit the country.

Chapter 8. The "Drink of Health"

Now that the benefits derived from the use of tea can be fairly estimated, it may be said, in the language of an eminent statesman: "what was first regarded as a luxury, has now become, if not an absolute necessity, at least one of our custom daily wants, the loss of which would cause more suffering and excite more regret than would the deprivation of many things which once were counted as necessaries of life."

Consumed by all classes, serving not simply as an article of diet, but as a refreshing and invigorating beverage, tea cannot be too highly estimated. The wisdom of successive financiers, and the enterprise of generations of merchants, have combined to deliver tea in this country at a price which brings it within the reach of every individual, making it, perhaps, the only real luxury which is common to rich and poor alike.

In noticing Dr. Johnston's work, entitled "The Chemistry of Common Life", the *Edinburgh Review* thus emphatically attests the great boon which tea confers upon the people.

It remarks: "by her fireside, in her humble cottage, the lonely widow sits; the kettle simmers over the ruddy embers, and the blackened teapot on the hot brick prepares her evening drink. Her crust of bread is scanty, yet as she sips the warm beverage – little sweetened, it may be, with the produce of the sugarcane – genial thoughts awakened in her mind; her cottage grows less dark and lonely, and comfort seems to enliven the ill-furnished cabin.

When our suffering and wounded soldiers were brought down frozen and bleeding from the trenches before Sebastopol to the port of Balaklava, the most welcome relief to their sufferings was a pint of hot tea, which was happily provided for them. Whence this great solace to the weary and worn? Why out of scanty earnings does the ill-fed and lone one cheerfully pay for the seemingly un-nourishing weekly allowance of tea? From what ever-open fountain does the daily comfort flow which the tea cup gently brings to the careworn and the week?"

Anon, referring to the chemical action of two important agents present in tea – theine[10] and volatile oil – the same excellent authority gives the following account of their operations on the human organism: "The theine is a substance possessing tonic or strengthening qualities, but distinguished particularly

---

[10] Theine is caffeine, 1,3,7-trimethyl xanthine.

by the property of retarding the natural waste of the animal body.

Most people are now aware that the chief necessity for food arises from the gradual and constant wearing away of the tissues and solid parts of the body. To repair and restore the worn and wasted parts, food must be constantly eaten and digested. And the faster the waste, the larger the quantity of food which must daily be consumed, to make up for the loss which this waste occasions.

Now, the introduction of certain quantity of theine into the stomach lessens the amount of waste which in similar circumstances would otherwise naturally take place. It makes the ordinary food consumed along with it, go farther, therefore, or, more correctly, lessens the quantity of food necessary to be eaten in a given time.

A similar effect, in a somewhat less degree, is produced by the volatile oil, and, therefore, the infusion of tea, in which both these ingredients of the leaf are contained, affects the rapidity of the natural waste in the tea drinker, in a very marked manner.

"As age creeps on, the powers of digestion diminish with the failing of the general vigor, till the stomach is no longer able to digest and appropriate new food as fast as the body wears away. When such is the case, to lessen the waste is to aid the digestive powers and maintaining the strength and bulk of the weakening frame.

'It is no longer wonderful, therefore,' says our author, 'that tea should be the favorite on the one hand, with the poor whose supplies of substantial food are scanty; and, on the other, with the aged and infirm, especially of the feebler sex, whose powers of digestion, and whose bodily substance have together begun to fail.'

Nor is it surprising that the aged female whose earnings are barely sufficient to buy what are called the common necessities of life, should yet spare a portion of her small gains in procuring this grateful indulgence. She can sustain her strength with less common food when she takes her tea along with it; while she, at the same time, feels lighter and spirits, more cheerful, and fitter for this dull work of life, because of this little indulgence".[11]

Such an indispensable article as tea has now become, ought to be trebly guarded against all

---

[11] *Edinburgh Review*, Vol. CI., No. 206, April 1855.

adulteration. While the government is unable capital is government to protect the public against the machinations of unscrupulous Chinese merchants, let the public at least endeavor to protect itself. And this it can readily accomplish.

Let it but bestow its custom on a trader upon whose integrity and technical knowledge it can implicitly rely. Let it insist upon having both its black and green teas of the natural hue, without the addition of "face", "glaze", or artificial color, which but detract from its character and value. How such a discrete selection can be affected has already been pointed out.

Houses of repute – such, for example, as that of Messrs. Horniman and Co. - do not conceal their names behind a retailer, but boldly give their own, coupled with a guarantee to every purchaser, however modest the purchase. Hence, consumers may feel assured that in buying indirectly from them, the commodity they obtain will not only be free from adulteration and artificial color but will be so carefully selected from the choicest growths, commensurate with the price demanded, as to be "always good alike".

Chapter 9. The Virtues of the Leaf

Dr. Lettsom, in a work published over a century since, avers that the infusion of tea possesses to peculiarities; the first a sedative quality, and the next, considerable stringency, by which the relaxing power is corrected so that the solids become strengthened and braced. Indeed, this writer goes so far as to pronounce tea far preferable to any other known vegetable infusion, if not drank too hot or into copious quantities, asserting that "if we take into consideration its known enlivening energy, our attachment to it will appear to be owing to its superiority in taste and effects to most other vegetables."

Dr. Edward Smith speaks of "the cup that cheers but not inebriates" as being a potent agent, and as increasing the quantity of carbonic acid emitted by the lungs and the quantity of air inspired, while at the same time it gives greater depth and freedom to the respiration.

"It is chiefly in its power", he remarks, "to increase the respiratory process that it asks so favorably, and in so doing the transformation of starchy and fatty food is promoted". Then he shows its vast advantages to the poor, by remarking: "In the dietaries of the poor, and where the meal must consist chiefly of bread, a substance not particularly savory, nor digested with great rapidity, the warm tea enables the recipient more readily to masticate and swallow the dry bread, or the bread with very little fat upon it, and so by its action to assist digestion."

The eminent Dr. Parkes avers that tea possesses a decidedly stimulative and restorative action on the nervous system, while, at the same time, it obviates succeeding depression.

This writer regards tea as a most useful article in cases of fever, when administered in the form of a cold, weak solution, and as being of great service to gouty subjects, and to those of a rheumatic tendency (especially such as labor under lithic acid diathesis) when drunk without sugar and with little milk.

Tea has been known to save life in cases of poisoning by tartar-emetic, the tannin being the active agent. Dr. Lewis's testimony also goes to support the medicinal importance of tea.

He mentions how it strengthens the stomach and intestines, is good against indigestion, nausea, and diarrhea, refreshes the spirit in heaviness and in sleepiness and counteracts the operation of inebriating liquors.

Some men of mark in their day were notorious for their tea-drinking predilections. Dr. Johnson himself may be fairly set down as a tea-gourmet. Then returning to more modern times, see how the genial Leigh Hunt bursts forth into rapture when describing the virtues of the beneficent plant, free from the cunning transformation practiced upon it by unprincipled traders.

Surely this gifted writer must have had a cup of Messrs. Horniman and Co.'s *spécialité* served to him when he could elaborate upon it thus:

"It was not green tea; it was not black tea; neither too young, nor too old; not unpleasing with astringency on the one hand, nor the insipid, half-earthy taste of decayed vegetable matter on the other; it was tea and in its most perfect state, full charged with aroma, which, when it was opened, diffused its fragrance through the whole apartment, putting all other perfumes to shame …….. Oh heavens! To sip that most exquisite cup of delight, was bliss almost too great for earth; a thousand years of rapture all concentrated into the space of a minute, as if the joy of all the world have been skimmed for my peculiar drinking, I should rather say imbibing, for to have swallowed that liquid like an ordinary beverage, without tasting every drop, would have been sacrilege."

Professor James F. W. Johnston likewise bears testimony to the value of this tropical beverage. He remarks:

"In the life of most persons a time arrives when the stomach no longer digests enough of the ordinary elements of food to make up for the natural daily waste of the bodily substance. The size and weight of the body, therefore, begin to diminish more or less perceptibly. At this time, tea comes in as a medicine to arrest the waist, to keep the body from falling away so fast, and thus to enable the less energetic powers of digestion still to supply as much is needed to repair the wear and tear of the solid tissues".

Of course, the chemical value of tea as a beverage depends upon the presence of volatile oil, theine, tannin, and gluten – the four substances forming its most important ingredients – and the proportions in which these exist.

If tea be not genuine, or if it undergoes the artificial process of coloring, its character and efficacy become proportionately impaired. It is unfortunately too true that the market is glutted with tea – which is either not tea at all, or else is excessively adulterated.

On the testimony of the House of Commons, "millions of pounds of sloe, licorice, and ash tree leaves, are every year mixed with Chinese teas for England". It is well-known that the leaves of the Chaparral, a Californian bush, are largely exported to China, when they return packed under the title of tea. A startling exposure was made a few years since, of the tea-rubbish styled "Finest New Season Kaisow", and "Fine Oanfa Congou", sold in bond at 1 1/4d. to 1 3/4d.[12] per pound.

Upon analysis the former was found to contain an enormous amount of mineral matter, chiefly iron filings; while the latter proved a mixture redried tea-leaves, straw, fragments of matting, rice husks, willow leaves, and the excrement of silkworms. The "Maloo Mixture", likewise, once gained an unenviable notoriety, as did the "Extra Fine Moyune Gunpowder" put up for sale by auction in Mincing Lane, and in

---

[12] Victorian money was divided into pounds (£) shillings (s. or /-) and pennies (d.). Thus, 4 pounds, eight shillings and fourpence would be written as £4/8/4d. or £4-8-4d. This would have ranged from 50 cents to one USD.

http://www.victorianweb.org/economics/currency.html

which Dr. Letheby discovered over 40% of iron filings in 19% of silica.

Tea is adulterated in two ways. The foreign dealers first practice their arts upon it by having recourse to dried leaves, and by "facing" – a process which necessitates the use of Prussian blue, silica, gypsum, plumbago, lamp-black, ferruginous earth, and other abominations.

Mr. Fortune, in his interesting work, reveals the whole secret. Upon reading his graphic account of how tea is elaborated for the European market, one almost turns aghast! And with good reason, as there might be ample cause to suspect "death in the pot".

Indeed, the people of China are themselves disgusted with the tricks of traders, who carry on their fraudulent practices without concealment. A Chinese Journal thus gives expression to the public sentiment:

"The wonder in that such stuff (referring to redried and recolored leaves) should be suffered to be manufactured, much less to be shipped as a lawful export, for Chinese law expressly prohibits the re--manipulation of tea that has once been used, on the obvious and common-sense principle that such a trade is necessarily, in its very essence, fraudulent.

Yet, in the face of this well-known maxim, it is one of the thousand proofs which we have of the utter rottenness of the present administration, that all around the settlement, and every convenient open space, large quantities of what is termed, with ominous propriety, the "mixture," lie exposed to the sun at noonday; in some cases, within 100 yards of the mixed court Yamen. And not only so, but there are establishments, well known to the police, where the mixture is fired, leaded, packed, sold, and dispatched for shipment; and experience has shown that it is useless to expect conviction, under Chinese law, from a Chinese magistrate".

The same journal, referring to a peculiar kind of willow which grows abundantly in the country, the leaves of which are utilized by tea manufacturers, observes:

"One needs not the expensive craft of the cha-sze to know how neatly a little skillful manipulation, and a little heat applied *secundum artem*, can transform these willow leaves into genuine and delicate tea leaves. Whether the mercantile result be intended to astonish the palates of old ladies in London or Glasgow, or to pass as genuine souchong with skippers, who have little knowledge of tea, we know not; but the fact remains, that the trade thrives well and pays.

"Nevertheless, there is still good and pure tea produced in China, and merchants in London who imported in an unadulterated condition, albeit a very large percentage of the 188,000,000 lbs. Annually consumed in Great Britain is spurious.

One mercantile firm in particular have gained a wide and well-deserved reputation for the purity and excellent character of their importations. I refer with pleasure to Messrs. Horniman and Co., London, who for nearly 40 years have assiduously labored to supply the public with both green and black tea, free from all mineral facing powder.

As what passes through the Wormwood Street Warehouses to their agents all over the country is subjected to no deteriorating and deleterious manipulation in China, its perfect purity can implicitly be relied upon. The Chinese letter which accompanied the first shipment, by Messrs. Horniman, of Tea into England, is quite original and unique. The translation reads thus: –

"The Flourishing Farm. – This is truly the very best tea, prepared with additional labor and free from coloring matter. The educated (or experienced) merchant, who is competent to consider it, will please to take notice of its clear and genuine quality. We are honored by your good orders and shall proceed at once to the packing".

The testimony afforded by several eminent analytical authorities in favor of Messrs. Horniman's importations is so satisfactory that nothing further can well be desired. The earliest of those documents is from Dr. Andrew Ure, F.R.S., Professor of Chemistry, who declares that upon chemical and microscopic examination of the samples taken from the bonded warehouses, he "found them (both black and green) to be perfectly free from all extraneous coloring matter, and in every respect genuine tea".

"Professor Ure further observes: – "The characteristic appearance of your green tea, namely the dull, olive hue, is unmistakably different to the bright blue tint of the ordinary green teas of commerce, which is artificially imparted.

This particular feature offers a perfect safeguard for the purity of the tea, in contrast with such sophisticated teas as I have sometimes been called upon to examine professionally for the Honorable Board of Excise, and which were coated with various powders that rendered them more or less unwholesome for use as an alimentary beverage".

Dr. Arthur Hill Hassall, Analyst of the County Sanitary Commission, and a well-known writer and authority on dietetics, after minutely describing the test to which he subjected the tea submitted to him for analysis, concludes in the following words: –

"These investigations enable me confidently to assume that the consumers of tea, now having fairly the choice of both the sophisticated and the pure, will not be slow in choosing between the wholesome natural kinds and those which are "got up" for appearance, and in order to realize higher prices through their defects being hidden or glazed over, with the powdered colors employed."

The latest report is from the same authority and bears a recent date. The opinion at first pronounced is therein but more strongly confirmed. The tea is characterized as being "perfectly pure, of superior quality, and free from facing".

Moreover, the packages which the analyst purchased from some of Messrs. Horniman's agents, he affirms, after careful examination, "to correspond as regards purity and excellence of quality with those teas obtained from the docks and from Messrs. Horniman's Wholesale Warehouses, in London".

Nor do authors and publicists of weight refrained from offering willing testimony in favor of Messrs. Horniman's special importation. Dr. Scoffern remarks how "Its delicious flavor fully confirms its entire freedom from the usual powdered color"; that he is "very partial to tea"; and that, in consequence of having long taken the pure beverage, his palate has become "the more critical".

The only certain way to obtain truly cheap and choice tea is to purchase the leaf without the usual mineral "facing" powder. That the public highly appreciate real economy is evident from the large and increasing trade carried on for the past 40 years by Messrs. Horniman & Co., the original importers of the pure tea.

Further, the agents of the firm throughout the kingdom, through Messrs. Horniman's direct operations, offer great advantages to the public, as they sell in the most distant neighborhoods the same reliable article, at the same fixed price, as their most extensive City or West-end agents.

In another article on tea consumption, appears the following: "Since the recent Parliamentary Report on Tea appeared, there has been a more general disinclination to use any that has been covered by the Chinese with mineral color, for this report exposed the fact that it is done to hide the brownness of wintry growths, and enable them, when so disguised, to be sold mixed off with the best at high rates.

From a lengthened experience I can bear testimony to the excellent and delicious character of Horniman's *pure tea*; while I am convinced that all who appreciate a strong, rich, full flavored beverage, possessing in addition a delicious flavor and aroma, must arrive at the light conclusion".

Chapter 10. A CUP OF TEA

What should mainly commend itself to our attention at the tea table, is the quality of the infusion. This is the crucial test. If the leaf be genuine, the proof is ready at hand. If otherwise, the proof is equally apparent, no matter how skillfully the leaf may be prepared to deceive the eye.

The pleasure of our morning and evening meal is much enhanced when the infusion is fragrant, lustrous, pleasant to the palate, and soothing to the nerves. Such covered herbal results, however, cannot be realized by those who, influenced by a false and flagrant economy, are led to purchase so-called "cheap teas", – noxious mixtures that in all probability have already done duty in Chinese teapots.

A lady of our acquaintance, while in the act of pouring out the grateful beverage, recently remarked, half apologetically: "What a very poor color this tea has! Either it must be uncolored, or else the Chinese have not put sufficient coloring matter on the leaf!"

To the inexperienced this remark naturally suggests the observation – "Do the Chinese really add "coloring" for the purpose of giving a deep color to the tea in the cup?" Be reassured then, gentle reader, and understand that the terms "colored" and "uncolored" are used to distinguish betwixt that tea which is painted or faced with mineral powder, principally Prussian blue and plumbago, and that which is *pure*, and free from any such prejudicial embellishments. A deep rich semitransparent infusion is always obtained from good and pure tea.

But for this popular error respecting the color of tea, I should scarcely have trenched on the precincts of the tea table – that forbidden ground where the housewife is universally regarded as the very model of perfection, and where her power, for the time being, is admittedly supreme.

The Chinese, whatever may be the character of the nefarious arts to which they resort to make the best of a bad commodity, can and do send us supplies of good tea. But then a fair price must be paid for it.

Such consumers of the beverage as are willing to procure genuine tea, and not lay out their money upon redried, rerolled, and "doctored" tea leaves, would do well to exercise judgment by selecting only those descriptions of tea that have been carefully plucked in the early spring, when the leaf is small and imbued with the richness of the shrub-juices.

Let but such a commodity be supplied perfectly uncolored, and the perfection of human art is attained. When the foolish fashion of the age required tea pretty to look at, then the Chinese, in deference to the public desire, and for the increased profits of those concerned colored or "faced" the leaf.

In conclusion, I may honestly aver that it is owing to the efforts of Messrs. Horniman that this reprehensible practice is fast falling into disfavor with the public. The enormous sale of the Firm's pure tea by some 4000 chemists, at once testifies to the high approval it has realized for its combinedly strong, delicious, and invigorating qualities.

John Horniman

[i]

[ii] **Horniman's Tea** is a brand of tea currently owned by Douwe Egberts https://en.wikipedia.org/wiki/Douwe_Egberts

The original tea trading and blending business 'Horniman's Tea Company' was founded in 1826 in Newport, Isle of Wight, by trader John Horniman. In 1852 he moved the company to London to be closer to the bonded warehouses of London Docks, then the biggest tea trading port in the world. Until 1826, only loose-leaf teas had been sold, allowing unscrupulous traders to increase profits by adding other items such as hedge clippings or dust. Horniman revolutionized the tea trade by using mechanical devices to speed the process of filling pre-sealed packages, thereby reducing his cost of production and hence improving the quality for the end customer. This caused some consternation amongst his competitors, but by 1891 Horniman's was the largest tea trading business in the world. - *Wikipedia*

Made in the USA
Columbia, SC
30 August 2019